For my love, Janet Lilo.

Beatnik Publishing

PO Box 8276, Symonds Street, Auckland 1150, New Zealand.

First published in 2021 by Beatnik Publishing

Text: © 2021 Courtney Sina Meredith
Editor & Introduction: Kim Meredith

Design, Typesetting and Cover design: © 2021 Beatnik Design Ltd.
Creative: Sally Greer
Typeface: Ashbury by Dieter Hofrichter & Ariata by Malou Verlomme
Endpaper Design: Sally Greer
Author portrait: Janet Lilo
Copyright of portrait photography remains with the photographer.

Printed and bound in China.

ISBN 978-0-9951180-9-6

BURST
KISSES
On The
ACTUAL
WIND

Courtney Sina Meredith

Beatnik

Contents

The great road north

If anyone had foreseen tree hugging in my future, I would have snorted with all the derision of a teenager who knows everything. Yet that's how your ascent into this world began, me your twenty-year-old mother staring at a tree outside the hospital window. The thickness of its trunk suggested strength, so I leaned into it during the waves of pain and began uttering slowly 'I am the tree and the tree is me.' You were an opportunity thrown from the heavens, as your youngest stepson would say. A fiery ball of small dark curls, skin pruned from sitting too long in my womb but already armed with a long list of requests for the journey ahead.

We began under a roof with three generations, in a rented wooden home, vegetables shooting from a garden toiled by my mother's hands in soil owned by the state. You were only two, dancing one night on the table, belting out Ardijah songs, hairbrush raised to your mouth and my parents seeing themselves in a way they never imagined. My father proclaiming, 'none of you were ever this way,' his eyes dancing with excitement, as though he sensed what was coming.

You must be so proud! This is how family, friends and even strangers greet me referring to the daughter who grew up to be a poet and writer and a champion of women of colour. The daughter who as a child loved basketball and collected baseball cards, who wrote songs melting people's hearts but mostly giving a voice to those silenced by circumstance. I would turn into my mother Rita and softly reply yes, of course I was very proud.

The families of my brothers and sisters have spent small fortunes buying coffee and fast foods waiting for the final call at Auckland airport as you headed out to Europe, the Americas, the UK, Asia, the Pacific and even Australia. Everyone says they want their child out in the world but once it happens you will never sleep again. You take calls in the middle of the night because they have lost their Oyster card, almost been mugged, had a fight with a lover or spent the last of the money you sent them for emergencies on organic blueberries and smoked salmon. There are flashes of your child having taken another path, a simpler one less taxing, no drama or excitement but it is too late because the time to turn around was never even an option. So you strap in and hold on tight, watch footage of her meeting members from the House of Lords, Presidents in faraway nations, Crown Princes from eastern regions, Muslim schoolgirls in Indonesia and wonder where, amidst this incredible journey, she will anchor.

I visited with family in Glen Eden, marvelling at the small stream that ran through the back of their yard. We laughed that it was like something out of a TV show from our childhood, not realising we were witnessing the very beginnings of the Whau River. The water making its way north, past neighbouring properties, through culverts, back out into the open before merging with a number of streams; the larger and more prominent being the Avondale and Whau streams, to become the enigmatic Whau River. A six kilometre stretch to reach the mouth between the familiar peninsulas of Te Atatu and Rosebank in Avondale, before rushing out to join the

Waitematā Harbour. For Māori the river was a rich vein, a life force that sustained them with native greens from its then lush banks, abundant kai moana from what was clean water, and an expressway between the Waitematā and Manukau harbours. They camped around the river mouth seasonally to cultivate food or to take a breather while passing through. Paddling waka up the river to the Avondale Stream, Māori carried these over a short stretch of land to Green Bay on the Manukau. I learned this is where Portage Road, which runs alongside the Avondale Stream, takes its name. Since it was an established boundary zone between tribal lands for centuries, intensive settlement arrived later in the form of migrants from the United Kingdom and Europe. The river and its streams faced a new era as an industrialised community placed near impossible demands on the waterways, but that's a story for another time.

If I backtrack from the mouth of the river, head south along the peninsula toward Avondale shopping centre, you arrive at an orange brick home sitting halfway up the slopes. There is a large plum tree nestled in the middle of the long narrow backyard, in summer the grass becomes littered with sweet fruit the kids readily scoop up. A small golden dog regularly patrols the top of the wooden fence line; from here I can easily retrace those steps, see the rooftops of houses spread out below, the intermediate and high schools, the strong thread of Rosebank Road and further beyond, cars ant-like follow one another down the Patiki Road onramp onto the north western, past wetlands teeming with bird and sea life, the Waitematā as always beckoning.

The sound of young voices carries through the open French doors, boys in the throes of fighting an online foe, the youngest singing at the dining table, painting fantastic lurid pictures. This is where I find you my daughter, where you have anchored. My daughter who travelled halfway around the world and back again. Under an endless sky along the main arterial of the great road north humming with life, this is where you found love and made a home in the heart of Avondale.

– Kim Meredith

I am aware of my privilege. Could y
I am aware of my privilege. Could y
aware of my privilege. Could y
of my privilege. Could y
my privilege. Could y
privilege. Could y
Could y
y

nnect me to a diverse community?
nnect me to a diverse community?
nnect me to a diverse community?
nnect me to a diverse community?
nnect me to a diverse community?
nnect me to a diverse community?
nnect me to a diverse community?
nnect me to a diverse community?
nnect me to a diverse community?
me to a diverse community?
to a diverse community?
a diverse community?
diverse community?
community?

Y

S scrubs the pots so give him Y
P was there so give him Y
X cleared her weekend so give her Y
S wants kids so give him Y
S stops calling unlikeable women 'bitches' so give him Y
P sends a text checking up on U
U miss him
P misses Y
X says that she dreams about Y
S fixes your car so give him Y
L is back from overseas
T is back with his wife
O comes home for a funeral
M turns up on opening night with B
S loves big dogs so give him Y
X is getting her shit together
X haunts U
P stops eating gluten
T emails his anxieties
O goes without a word
S pats you back to sleep
P keeps your secret
X drifts further and further
S tells his Nan he met someone
U are harvesting Y
U are holding it to your chest

How about being a woman?
How about being a young woman?
How about being a young brown woman?
How about being a young brown queer woman?
How about being a young brown queer single woman?
How about being a young brown queer single educated woman?
How about being a young brown queer single educated professional woman?
How about being a young brown queer single educated professional creative woman?
How about being a young brown queer single educated professional woman?
How about being a young brown queer single educated woman?
How about being a young brown queer single woman?
How about being a young brown queer woman?
How about being a young brown woman?
How about being a young woman?
How about being a woman?

I keep my own hours

I write on the side

I take it easy on myself

I make excuses

I follow the rules

The law of nature

The loss of appetite

I come undone

Just like you

I sit in the long grass

I take my time

I take notes

In lectures

At readings

In lieu of feeling

I take notes

I cite wars

Just like you

I open my arms

I follow through

I know the script

We are reading from

I sit by the river

I pick every petal

The river loves me

The river doesn't love me

Just like you

Homeland

You get back everybody says oh you're back!
You are back but everything has moved.
You are an old woman
you are a concrete crow you are a set of lilac limbs.

Everybody says tell me about somewhere?
You are the plentiful remains of war fought towns.
You get to sleep one night and then the next.
Everybody thinks you dream in foreign prose.

Everybody knows you are back.
Everybody sees your body in the city in the arms of friends.
You are a silver canal
you are a young rose you are a path grown men skate.

Everybody stands in front of you like a mirror.
They do their hair in your face *so good you're back!*

You are certain in the seeing of what appears whole.
You are a nought you are a track you are a bone.

You are waiting to come home.
You are waiting to come home.
You are waiting to come home.

I watch your hair passing mountains
I watch the colours fade

> houses cut into rock
> the animals there know home
> waters dead in thicket

> you are a bird
> I keep you sung
> in my rib cage.

Why do you get all Waikato blue?
Why do you burn our churches?

One day I will take you
back to where I came from

lay down cliff
northern star: purple Cortina

> emerald yonder
> bull rush lilies.

> Do you remember
> what it was? Shiny fracture

small unread. Platinum
sun crossed grass.

> I don't remember
> how this room came to be

whose hands under your soft neck
believe it rests inside.

Magellanic Clouds

Location:	Avondale at sunset
Players:	2
Talanoa:	Orbiting the Milky Way
Album:	The National, Trouble Will Find Me
Hors d'oeuvres:	Ready salted kettle chips
Obstacles:	Manifold
Allegretto:	A little joyful
Narration:	On dark nights you can see two irregular dwarf galaxies with your naked eye/ visible in the southern celestial hemisphere/ they reach their highest point in January/ a myriad of star clusters/ nebulae/ at opposite ends of the living room/ not kissing

eye

drove to your house parked across the road   'm n town
'm selfish   know   'm sorry
ddn't get out   wanted to   chckened out
sold everythng   gave up smokng   took up Jesus
went to Caro   wanted to rng   ddn't thnk enough tme had passed
mssed your voce   wasn't n New York   wanted to say sorry
know   don't deserve your tme   know   hurt you   .
ddn't mean to   had ths dea   was somewhere else   was wrong
wasn't n Pars   ran out of cash n Morocco   got work n a town wth no name
cleaned rooms   poured drnks   worked lke a dog
wrote to you   never sent the letters   burnt them n a feld
took pctures of the smoke   mssed your laugh   went to Rome
lt a candle at the baslca.   prayed for you   sent my love·
know   should've prayed for myself   .

20

X—X—
X—X—

Cowboy

Did you know that emotions have farewells?

They have lovers and birthdays
their own secret ambition

Whole lives

Most of my emotions lead full lives

      Some of my emotions have low self-esteem
      I want them all to move away and then I

      remember the sharp edges of the sky
      if you reach too high you will be cut

You ask me all the time if I'm happy

      I feel you asking in your spending
      in the long hours smoothing out

      my wild name

All the time asking what I'm thinking
and are there speaking parts in this movie?

      the women are weakened by love
      and the broken men carry pistols

      there is an eye of god that sounds
      exactly like a drunken cowboy

You want to know your lines
and where to stand when the spirit moves

      I cannot tell you where they run to
      but some emotions never return

      even if you send perfumed letters
      hoping the scent of their mother

      will be enough

      it is never enough

      for some

the night sky is an immigrant
coming from somewhere unknown

half the group went into the past
where the food was good and the coffee was hot
but not you and me we made our way
into thick dust beyond the merry-go-round
both of us joking about children
if only we had them to make excuses
it takes mystery and cunning to do that
you said with your gaze on a dead canvas
this is where the artist goes to die
something that wasn't in the statement
you said the lives you tried on never seemed to fit
especially the one that waited at home
some of the group came back sick of war
the one you loved best went into the future
we saw him by the car on its side downstairs
with his pale hands smooth on the bonnet
that was real life that was contemporary
he told you he only slept with distant women
so you stayed with me in the present
perhaps for the rush of complicity
to oppose yourself until time overlapped
outside your eyes slid through wet leaves
beyond the flat field and its buzz of death
enough to see his long and distant form
you said it was the earth peeling away and not us

Burst-kisses-on-the-actual-wind
Lose-my-shit-the-closest-to-God
Mean-to-tell-you-I-want-you-bad
Mention-instead-something-dumb
An-irrelevant-random-acquaintance
Tell-the-girls-nothing-act-cool
Date-regularly-forget-their-names
Smile-talk-about-the-mahi-sweat
Give-my-body-permission-to-fall
Open-toed-wedges-at-the-BBQ
Watch-the-sun-watching-you
Learn-the-names-of-your-kids
Circle-your-tā-moko-with-my-eyes
Hang-the-washing-say-no-prayer

PONY

New Lynn
Actually, a whole travelling farm - a portable farm - with rats and bunnies, chickens too? It was my sister's birthday.

Baths
Unless my memory is playing tricks on me. The rats were white with blazing red eyes.

I'm translating myself from a time
when I was sure.

      Sex with strangers
The man leading the pony in circles was wearing a cowboy hat.

           Sunday School
There was a big pink cake with purple icing and sprinkles.

Of being outside
I was too big to ride the pony. By then I was a young woman.

           Conflicts with a certain city
Loads and loads of animals. The smaller children took turns riding the pony around the backyard. There was a creek beyond the section.

I see flashes of our father
up to his knees in dirty water.

Lost love
My sister's name written in M&Ms

      and he is smoking fish and you will be left behind.

Aso fanau

Some family friends gave me an authorised portrait of
Mandela for my birthday.

A girl made me a necklace. I kept it for a long time.
I think I still have it. I can't find my passport.

I had a high tea. My cousin came late with a stir-fry.
My present is under her bed. A drawing. She says it has to
be perfect.

I grew by accident. One moment I was wordless
the next I was toasting myself under a washing line.

I made a big curry for all of my friends.
One of them gave me Twenty Love Poems and a Song of
Despair.

My cousin went to see another friend at a bar. A guy
asked them for a threesome. They said no.

I read about Nelson when everybody left.

Blue-crowned lorikeet
can do no wrong she
eats the lung of the niu she
nests in the holes of trees
orange bill yellow eye
purple thigh opaque abdomen
red throat she only exists
in the mind of a little rain
cannot reference an indeterminate
change no she inhabits heat
it has always been, the flowering
point of yonder. She eats
nectar pollen small eyes
including wild hibiscus. She
came to me when I was within reach
most stay tame most stay tame!

Smoke

home all day   you sit at the edge of the living room
on your best behaviour   man   cat   fire   two winds appear
            who will win   your body asks
sinking deeper   into carpet
                                but time but cars   pass
        the contract   eats itself   and I stay in my skin

your body is wet when you're sad
            I lie at the centre   a pool of oil
If I answer this call   will the smoke rise?
                                are the ancestors
        always watching?

this is my   other
                the quiet half   eaten alive

1

1 x mother
1 x 'father'
1 x shooting star

Mecca

Supper on Durham Lane
talking backstroke
getting further   spot on the pounamu horizon
a mate told me how to detail oblivion
it depends if you are sitting or standing
it depends on the height of the ship   getting further
gold hair in your eyes   Mayfair Kuwait a chopper
first thing in the morning
my brother got a bite on the hand (dog)
your family sounds like a film set!   So far
it took three of us and two trolleys to feed the family
   a curry goes far   a cole-slaw stretches
his living room is painted by the blood of history
(dye-fig/ insatiable bark)

during the voyages of migration
nobody could harpoon
the horizon

she was a woman
heard laughing always
in the next room under water
mountain side she was
never where you were.

Household Gods

Household Gods have gotten hold of the remote
we are forced to watch Survivor
with the volume as high as the ear will go.

Unlike general Gods
drag racing down our street
the art of defining a centipede
from a bag of wheat is like
advising revolution
where flesh is weak.

There is no cure
but aromatic flowers high in a tree
you need a limber boy
to pick them with his teeth.

There is no remorse
but the juice of immature fruit
ground with beetle wings and breast milk.

When prayers fail
so too does the body.

If the Lord is angry
ankles of a deaf women straighten
she is drowned with description
that won't translate.

The capital God believes
tears from a pilgrim –
languid grief
can steer the soul to self.

Love is a resurrection

We drive down Ponsonby Road and turn into a memory
I know this place
        my blood is in the soil
my elders have a pact with this land
        I was conceived not far from here
if you found my father you could mention
            the bend of this reserve and he would know
   the paths by rote

                it surprises you
                how married I am to this place
there is so much earth to unfold between us
there are suns beyond the sun we can feel

you walk around pretending to be new   but love is a resurrection
            divinity by accident   the hot matter coursing
under your skin under my skin

                    if you close your eyes

our love will reach behind the stars

                     if I close my eyes

my father will return to me and your father will return to you

Ielusalema

Elijah plants a tree, thinks he sees mum
his dead mum moving like seaweed in bloom
in front of his house there a palm-like tomb
is open for all hands and wings to come
praise his mother in tapa, like a nun.
She has no children no burgeoning swoon
of flies and men to brush like morning dew
from shoots too small underfoot where blood runs.
Lately the sun has set the garden pink
when he pulls in from work with his girlfriend
the backyard dirt feels like grains of concrete
no water, beer, or piss the soil will drink.
They make love in the kitchen and deaden
his mother's voice, so drowned by lives complete.

va'a   ship   constellations
spirit world
patterns?
dimensions   micropause
aroha (collective)   flow
connections
untangling teu
to keep the space
to tidy up the space
to adorn the space
to look after the space
unending?

Land's End

The Ks are high, the Ks are low
but the seats are uncomfortable
oh spaghetti, couldn't have that:
he's Arabian on the hustle
trying to make ends meet
I wrap a hand around, both ways
could the dog fit – and the shine
would they laugh me out of Run Club?

Is this really the best price in the city
the best price in New Zealand in fact
he mutters hosing down the silver hole
black hole really, money guzzler

may as well open my window
push out the French doors throw
everything I saved to live off
only to come to a head, land's end

unfair, whatever you're saving
can't be a lifelong raft, life insurance,
I made an enquiry, but I'll never know
twirling in the hot earth... Presume
whoever I chose knows, what colour
brings out my eyes

then again, they'll be closed...

He rings an hour later says, thick accent,
and it's hurting his throat all the way:
a hundred dollars off my dear

because you know, he's made a loss
and I must've looked around of course –
made a point of searching
similar creatures, adequate plots

had I not imagined
having to compromise
one day, finally?

Silence, awkward pause
god I spent hours thinking about this moment
there's a history on my Mac to prove it
so I can't go forgetting, what I've lost.

Petrol is cheap but house prices are soaring
you have to pay your respects to the roof
over your head, before it spins
into the sun.

November in New York

I hear the term 'liberal elite', and the bird inside my chest
stops singing. Goes quiet. Plays dead.

I wonder when the music will come back?

Meanwhile, the clothes need washing and there's two girls
at the door wanting to eat something like what they've
seen in the movies.

Hotdogs, pizza, burgers as big as your head. They want to
drink cosmopolitans like Carrie and her girlfriends,
fuck strangers and stay up all night high on life.

I let them in and we read together, in silence,
while the small sun goes to bed,
folding itself into the side of a skyscraper.

Remember when you were with a woman?

Remember how you went everywhere together?
And how being with a woman made you think
You had a right to wear your leathers every day
Wearing your leathers to the mall
At the funeral in your leathers
Shining in your leathers pumping gas
Walking to the dairy in your leathers
Hanging washing in your leathers
Returning library books in your leathers
Hiding in your leathers drinking decaf
Running from the rain in your leathers
Remember telling me that she babysat the wild in you?
Remember saying that being with a woman
                          was like crawling back into the earth
And how being with a woman made you think
                              that you must be really deep
And how being with a woman made you think
                              that you were never deep enough
And there was a part of you that wanted to claim her like a new moon
And there was a part of you that wanted to run
Remember telling me that her body was so beautiful
So beautiful it scared you
You said loving her was like trying to put your arms around the sea
You said loving her was like dipping your heart in salt water
You said she was a much better woman than you would ever be

Remember?

Shower head / drip drip drip
Neighbours / get inside kids
Pink flamingo / doesn't move
Office plants / take up space
4 3 2 1 / half-read
Blinds / clank intermittently
Girlfriend / don't go on and on
Sunhat / paralysed
Crystal tree / waning red
Washing machine / distant hum
I / go on and on

Corner

       'I didn't say that
        it's not sexy. The first thing I said in German was
        I am feeling hot, and do you take drugs?

they took me at night break
angry at the system
angry at the egg white sky
wheaten neck of lion (mane)
rock gone orange
grass gone brown

       can you score me some Persian elixir?

they know everything
angry at female math
angry at the undone town
malting in the square
feather spindrift'

The internet told me to go for a run
I walked to the park with good posture
The sky asked me to catch it while it fell
I opened my arms to their maximum
The house said it needed a vacuum
I loaded the dishwasher and turned it on
The silence wanted its throat slit
I sang to myself while I made dinner

Twin Goddesses

I'm in a game collecting paper
TV, power, phone, loan, insurance.

And she's like
      write the country down
And I'm like
      hello *Italy!*
And she's like
      where is Umbria?
And I'm like
      are you serious?

Pink, yellow, blue notes,
in leather, in secret.

And she makes me declare myself
write a price on bright green paper
it looks cheap – love,
from this distance.

And I'm like
      is this real?
And she's like
      look around!
And the twin goddesses call
      Taema holds my hand
And the room fills with sky
      Tilafaiga holds my wing.

Gold, orange, white notes,
in exile, in a furnace.

And she's like red hotels
And she's like plastic rocks
And she's like whale's teeth
And she's like the lost song
And the words burn in salt.

Held

Lay down or declare or exist in something permanent
they never get tired of petri dish rhetoric
setting halves setting wounds

likened old warm body
like Hotere or the cross
armed guard or Niue
or women of Yemen
burning their veils

identity is a luxury
found in bright street chants
backyard fire amber glitter
alight! We are weaving our people into life
young hands milking the flowering son
his stars his holographic promise
young fe'e young partridge.

Iowa House Hotel

In a dream last night we agreed on a course of action.
Here is our true north, said the actors playing you and I.
They shook hands.

One cooked for the other, one did the dishes, they
measured their freedom by square metres.

In another dream to a soundscape of elevator jazz, they
found each other in a bar overseas.

You looked so much like you, so much as I remember.

The bartender said, what'll it be? You asked for wine, the
person playing me asked for gin, typical.

Outside, because it was kind of London and kind of
Jerusalem and sort of Chicago, the sky was a mash-up of
glitter constellations.

Whoever you almost were in the dream – some voice
inside a code of scents –
tricked my mind.

You looked so much like you, so much as I remember.

Mexico City

Fabric markets/ piñatas hanging on the side of buildings/
chilli and bean eggs on the terrace/ the idea of a neon
memory/ Yusef Komunyakaa across from me at dinner/
in a smart jacket chatting to Carolyn Forché/ they are
grand masters/ tomorrow we will visit the home of Frida
Kahlo/ red wine and cactus spirits/ tomorrow we'll see
the soft place Frida fell when the pain was all too much/
was love her greatest pain/ I think/ on the way to my
reading I passed three churches with their doors wide
open/ pews exposed/ wooden ribs/ you can learn the
science of people who just talk/ alongside people who
just act/ there is a bright line/ everybody says yes/ but
only some people move/ this is the festival circuit/ a
made place we think up collectively/ breezily/ stone
house/ machete.

I have stolen away into the secret room

mothers build inside their daughters

I am feeding on a dowry centuries old

the bones sucked dry

a feast of bright quiet.

My mother's dreams are here

beside the red gold river

born of shame and laughter

the shifting bank won't hold.

Her mother's wings are here

wild shimmered iridescent

girl to bird to prophet

an angel killing time.

And there is her mother

at the top of the sky ablaze

lighting the islands below

into a string of tears.

Mile End

We go past some houses in the night
it's a blue night no rain houses sway
past the train it's a clear night

one stood footballer
covered in the field around the corner
eyeballs me

Piccadilly
open night. Allow the light
should light arrive.

King's Cross pancreas
acute
boy spit
part word anthem:
step out with me Lucy?

He calls it the perfect storm. Imagine the world in 80
years.
Please ask questions. Peter mentions a problem
do you want to know what the challenge is? Polish beauty
asleep on the table beside me
eats her chestnut curls.

I pour a little orange
do my best to believe
in Matt with his lazy tongue
circling wide oyster
auē he can't flick it fast enough! A woman controls her
own body
these days.

Rhythm method. Pull out.

Identity is a dangerous God

How can we eliminate the bloodletting –
do we want to? Bearded omen lashing
cream. Isn't the Oxford sun inhuman?

Identity is a dangerous God.

Brian will resurrect his significance
Brian will rescue his poignance
Brian will overcome Nabokov for Popper
Brian will get to the heart of it.

Scientific laws are permanently changing. There is no certain knowledge.
You cannot recapture the past. Old boy
looks to the moon
ages me consistently. Science is not a new God
throws me under melting willow
I expect to end there
recounting my white swan.

I was having a conversation with you
when Chicago came along and my heart panged
for a group of wolves you'll never meet
I spent a lot of time in darkened rooms looking at art
also Chernobyl as Hyperborea beyond the north wind

I ordered chocolate chip pancakes for the table
that's something international women do
that's something I learned to do
behaviours are like accents

They order food for inanimate objects
women with money
women with power

All the while tracking constellations as truth
as though our bodies as night skies are capable of that
that much light

It's the sound of a place you've absorbed
your tongue splits to make room
for the new selves that bloom
and you are talking
almost cheerfully
when it hits

meaalofa

we make love to a mixtape of cicadas and falling stars
you have a house and a good job
my new car has very low k's

we sit across from each other at right angles
your sister in law is calling again
my sister is back on Waiheke

we talk about the future in morse code
the fucker is coming for us
quick wave a white flag

we are so many things outside of this room
your father is the twinkling shark king
my father is running through the jungle

we undress each other slowly
bodies of water in the moonlight

29

i
I traced you little taboo little unstuck southern cross
but you already knew you already knew
who belonged to who.

ii
It's been so long since I knew dry land
or stood among the sooty loved
greasy in a selfless gape.

iii
Another good friend sends a message
about permanent employment
and the possibility of agricultural volunteering.
I can't see myself picking olives
in the red shade.

Commonly misspelt words

Allowed disappeared holidays stopped
awhile doesn't hopped straight
believe dollars hospital they're
breakfast don't instead threw
brought everybody lightening tomorrow
cannon everyday luckily video
can't everywhere nearly wasn't
caught excited police watch
centre favourite present weren't
chocolate field probably we're
clothes friends quiet whole
couldn't front scared won't
didn't grabbed second you're
different having someone.

As a woman
is it okay to like petals?

A woman
in front of gold petals

look, her eyes are shut

sometimes I think

'this one looks better
this version right here'

inflamed in leather

saying sorry

for no particular reason

sorry, I avoided conflict

and took up many causes

some of them women
most of them men

a sea monster whose wounds
matched my own

look, look
it's a woman

covered in gold

Aroha Mai

Aroha mai
I was trying to get to you
but the wind kept changing direction

Aroha atu
she hates it when institutions use Te Reo in their signatures
she hates it when my wet hair drips all over the bedsheets

Aroha mai
I couldn't see you this time
I was down a rabbit hole
along the coast beside the point

Aroha atu
love given love received
there isn't enough room in this house to house our love
the brick square flat beneath a rectangle sky

Aroha mai
your baby finally came
the angels found your address submerged in yesterday's current
and she's clapping in every photo

Aroha atu
my feet don't touch the ground these days
I take the stairs to stay fit
I keep my car full of gas
it is easy to recycle the past

Aroha mai
my ghost is in town
and I don't know if I should email her back

Aroha atu
already the skeleton wings of this year are casting long shadows
we don't know what's for dinner but next door's
Tūī keeps singing all the buried bones to life
and you're opening every can of beans in the cupboard
to feed the tired warrior in my arms

Today was Thanksgiving I lay in bed feeling crappy, picturing the moon, beaming in some other part of the world, calling my womb home. I thought about leaving the house but I couldn't move, there was nothing about my body that made any more or any less sense than usual. I wanted to see my mother and cry into her shadow. I wanted to be some place warm and free of longing. I wanted to buy sea salt and hot sauce. I wanted to bench press spiritual cargo. I wanted all my questions answered by a higher power. The quilt got cooler, my legs stopped kicking. I gave up for an hour. Later in the day when the darkness took a blue tinge and the mountains made up for the quiet (because, you know, your voice can only carry so far), I ate frozen berries in bed. My body got cooler. I pictured the sun, beaming in some other part of the world.

Honolulu

1. Shuttle bus to the shops at Waikiki.

2. Soaked from head to toe in the burger bar.

3. Full colour Diamond Head.

4. VIP bus around town.

5. A lone cruise ship in the distance floats by.

6. Taxidermy polar bear next to warriors.

7. Anxiety picnic in the sunshine.

8. Another deadline another cruise ship.

9. Wings in teeth.

10. Eyes shiny with tears.

of all the bricks we laid in our sleep

asleep I built the motorway

collectively most cemeteries

it kept us glowing darling

among the chosen ones

back stroke I swam back

with a mouth full of mud

to see the stars we broke

and hear your soft waiata

through the floorboards

Smoking in the garden
One hand in your pocket
Our little dog curling
Herself around your feet
The closing day pictures
You in a concrete cloud
Missing a friend out of town
Maybe missing yourself too
Turning in navy linen
Eye level with the gods
On our sloping lawn

Drive silent streets
1am cuppa with the ancestors
2am toilet visit
3am indiscriminate whirring
4am ...
5am rainfall
6am birdsong
7am yoga

Grandpa Green Bananas

It's Grandpa's birthday today

We Skype while he shows me his breakfast

The boiled ribcage of a small chicken

Animated on paper towels

His fingers work the nooks

Tearing flesh from cartilage

While his eyes fill with tears

While my eyes fill with tears

On a romantic stroll to an empty gallery
The streets like the contents of a Raro sachet
Everyday grit glitter and distanced walkers
We spied a tiger blanket on a communal washing line
Where you said the residents had moved on
Like the one who ran with knives
And the one who suffered from social anxiety
But there was the silent offering in the wind
Betraying whatever survivor survived

Our dreamer comes home

The wind warms itself to be close to him

Every bird that should be soaring stops to sing

All the wishes of all the sons nobody ever had

Shrink down from a dam into a teacup

And there he is long-limbed on the couch

Talking to a friend about the next 20 minutes

Deliciously oblivious to his eternity

I like real she says
I like the truth

Her real sisters turn up
Both of them

One with her little girl
One in a white van

The neighbours watch from their windows

We stay in a bubble on the front lawn
waving like maneki-neko

It's better when you're honest she says
Instead of drinking wine and smiling

With her real hands on the real sun while the
neighbourhood goes dark

On Monday my lover lost her keys
They were found in a jacket pocket

On Tuesday she lost her sunglasses
Several new pairs were bought

On Wednesday I lost all hope
In the supermarket car park

I wanted to faint but the world turned upside down

On Thursday I had 4 video conferences in a row
The voices and the faces wouldn't sync

And everybody's bright ideas didn't matter anyway

We were lost little children outrunning the monster
And then it mattered very much who could act

On Friday I explained speech act to the children
I was promising and I was warning but not fearing

On Saturday we stopped counting the dead
My lover painted the back room lilac

It was almost like a day from the past

Too much folk music in the kitchen
Careful the steak will be too depressed to dance in our
bellies tonight

The deseeded chilli will fade from red to grey
And the lotatoes won't strive for the light

I've let the mascarpone loose
Tonight is as good a night as any

And anyway I've forgotten the ritual we decided on
Defining our soundtrack as 'ultimate pop'

Too many e's tuned to d too many southern drawls
I've lined our Polynesian sanctuary with anguished white
men

They're wailing to the moon in between whisky and texts
to estranged exes
They're filling my head with so many artificial rivers

To find me you'll need as many empty barrels
As barrels filled with hopefuls
Going over Niagara

STOP SENDING POEMS

I had an ex that couldn't spell
he blamed it on being bilingual
I never knew if he could spell
in that other language

He used to pat me to sleep
like I was a new calf
and he was the soft grass
lame in my mouth

I tried to send him a poem but the ink refused
drained to the bottom of the page and sat there
clumped together in one rebellious night
without stars

I had been alone for too long
sitting in air-conditioned halls
retracing my steps
reimagining the shore
crumbling backwards

whales eating cars eating waves
swallowing tables covered in paper and coffee
until my legs dangled in the salted froth

I never got to send the ocean my sonnet
about Vailima mermaids at Long Bay

Stop sending a message to the omniverse
as though you have a direct line
Stop praying with your mouth open the flies will get in
Stop agonising over tiny details the tiny deaths of chances never taken
Practical council workers take missed chances to a farm
They grow old and fat under the sun with many siblings
Stop equating newness with perfection! screams the skyline
Pocked with hired cranes as far as the eye can strain
The cranes are controlled by young men

The cranes are owned by old men
You are all dots on rotation! shouts the poem

I never got to undress you with my limited but expensive longing

The shop girls in New York sprayed it on a card and let it waft
they told me to walk through it and I did as I was told
Oh the sweetness and the citrus

for you I am draining the bottle
for you I am forgetting my scent

I had an ex who loved the idea of me so much she would sit
uncomfortably on the bach fence for reception
waiting for that one twinkling bar to read my texts
littered with metaphors and golden omens
how I longed to be with her on the cowhide rugs

I sent her complicated conversations with myself
arranging chaos and beauty conveniently
the gigs I was going to and the men
I merged into one big moon face

I sent a letter to the editor as a child asking for less corny car ads
I rang a radio station and rapped to win a bag of jellybeans
my favourite colour is none of your business!
goes the poem

I meant to send you an email about a memo wearing a contract
My heart was in its cage on the floor eating lettuce
I had been fattening her up during a fairytale winter
One that goes on for many years while the villagers wait for help
I started taking her to work in my handbag
Letting her nibble on memories under my desk

I was ending my official information act to you with warmest regards
I was entering the birthdates of human rights for your information
My eyes were fixed on the first term and the final condition
A report with the face of a thesis and the body of a song
I was adding my digital signature and pressing send
When my heart –

Avondale Heights

You knock on the door for the hundredth time,
only this time your children are waiting outside.
I'm going to get a key cut for you tomorrow.

I open the door and you're smiling.

A big smile. My smile.

I've booked us all tickets to see the Lion King at LynnMall
this afternoon.

Behind your smile you're hiding seven hours of getting
the boys ready for soccer, driving to far flung muddy
fields, standing at different sidelines chanting their
names.

I walk down the steps behind you. I can see them talking
to each other in the car.

The horizon is vast.

Fa'afetai tele lava

My editor for this collection and beloved mother, Kim Meredith... x

My publisher for this collection and dear friend, Sally Greer... x

My inspiration for this collection and truest love, Janet Lilo... x

My village for this collection and treasured aiga... x

My children for this collection and everlasting alofa... x

Courtney Sina Meredith

Courtney Sina Meredith is a distinguished author
whose work delves into issues such as racism, sexism
and poverty. Her debut poetry collection *Brown Girls
in Bright Red Lipstick* (Beatnik, 2012) was followed by
acclaimed short story collection *Tail of the Taniwha*
(Beatnik, 2016), and historical feat *The Adventures of
Tupaia* (Allen & Unwin, 2019).

Courtney has been awarded prestigious creative
opportunities around the world. Heralding an era of
niu leadership, her heart lies in giving voice to the
contemporary experiences of Moana fafine.

The descendant of ancestors from Samoa, Mangaia and
Ireland, she lives in her hometown of Aukilani, Aotearoa
with partner visual artist Janet Lilo, and their children.

Where I am now in my life is
where I've been for a very long
time – inside the wave. As a writer
and performer, I've had the great
blessing of documenting the sea
salt, struggles, genetic memory and
enduring ambition from within our
Moana communities.

— Courtney Sina Meredith